BODYSCOPE

Brain Box

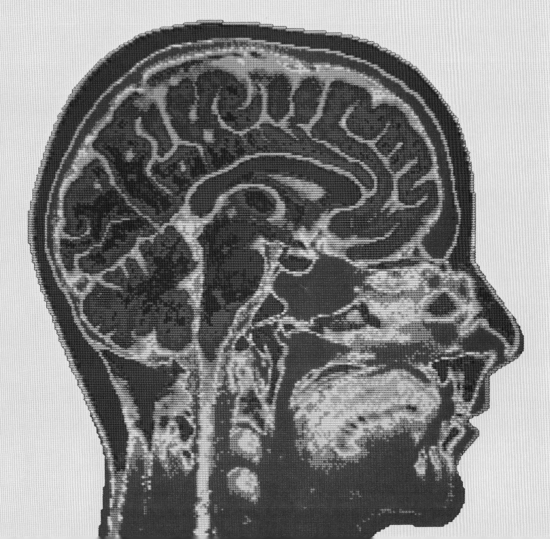

BODYSCOPE

Brain Box

The brain, nervous system and senses

Dr Patricia Macnair

Consultant:
Richard Walker

KINGFISHER

KINGFISHER

Kingfisher Publications Plc,
New Penderel House,
283–288 High Holborn,
London WC1V 7HZ
www.kingfisherpub.com

First published by Kingfisher
Publications Plc 2005
10 9 8 7 6 5 4 3 2 1
1TR/0205/PROSP/PICA(PICA)/140MA/C

ISBN-13: 978 0 7534 0968 8
ISBN-10: 0 7534 0968 2

A CIP catalogue record for this book
is available from the British Library.

Printed in China

Author: Dr Patricia Macnair
Consultant: Richard Walker
Editor: Clive Wilson
Designer: Peter Clayman
Illustrators: Sebastian Quigley, Guy Smith
Picture researcher: Kate Miller
Production controller: Lindsey Scott
DTP coordinator: Carsten Lorenz
Indexer: Sue Lightfoot

Contents

Control centre

▲ You need precise and rapid finger movements to play the harp. The brain controls every one of these movements.

Every movement, every thought and every feeling you experience is controlled by your nervous system. This is made up of your brain, spinal cord and a network of nerves. The nervous system is always switched on – even when you are asleep, millions of signals are travelling along the nerves.

Central station

Together, the brain and the spinal cord form the central nervous system. This is the body's main control centre. Cable-like nerves carry messages between the central nervous system and the rest of the body.

The natural order

The brain works out what movements the body needs to make and what order they should follow. It then sends out commands to the muscles through the nerves.

◄ This boy's body is not moving, but his brain is hard at work. The brain uses up large amounts of energy.

▲ Signals travelling around the nervous system reach speeds of up to 350km/h. This makes them even faster than the super-quick Japanese Bullet train.

Outside information

In order to control your body's movements, your brain needs to know what is happening in the world around you. Information comes in from the sense organs. These include your eyes, ears and even your skin.

brain

spinal cord

◀ Instructions from this boy's brain pass down the spinal cord and along the nerves to different parts of his body. These signals control the muscles that allow him to keep his balance.

Communication

Most animals can communicate with each other but only humans, with our complex brains, have highly developed languages. With speech and writing we can share our thoughts and feelings, and work together. We also use other signals, from facial expressions to body posture, all controlled by the brain.

nerve

▶ These Egyptian picture-signs are an example of hieroglyphics — one of the world's oldest forms of writing.

Inside the brain

Your brain is packed with tiny nerve cells called neurons. A piece of brain the size of a grain of sand contains 100,000 neurons! These neurons connect up to make your brain the most powerful and intelligent machine in the universe.

▲ The outer layer of the brain has a huge number of folds. This allows a lot more of it to fit inside the skull.

Grey matter

The outer part of the brain, which does your thinking, is called the cerebral cortex, or grey matter. Its folds give the brain a wrinkled look. Below the grey matter, millions of neurons carry signals between different parts of the brain.

It's all relative

You do not need a big brain to be a genius! Albert Einstein's brain was smaller than an average person's. People who are very intelligent may simply be using their brain in a different way.

skull protects the brain

cerebellum controls muscle movement and balance

breathing is controlled by the brain stem

▶ The brain has three main areas — the cerebrum, the cerebellum and the brain stem.

◀ Albert Einstein made amazing scientific discoveries, but his brain was on the small side!

8

Special protection

Because the brain is soft and delicate, it needs to be protected. The brain floats in a layer of fluid, which cushions it inside the skull. The bones of the skull provide the brain with a natural crash helmet.

cerebrum controls language, thought and movement

Messenger system

Neurons carry electrical signals around the brain and also the body. They come in all shapes and sizes. Although most neurons are no longer than a full stop, some are the longest cells in the body, stretching from your toe to your spine.

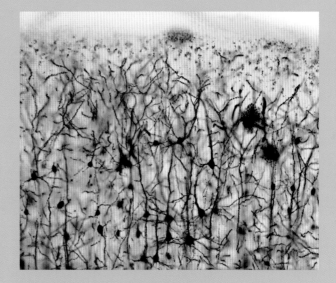

▲ These black dots are neurons. Each one is connected to hundreds and sometimes thousands of other neurons.

Active brain

Your brain is in charge of your body – it's the boss! Different parts perform different tasks. Some areas receive information, others send out messages to the muscles. The brain also has areas to process information so that you can think, remember and make plans for the future.

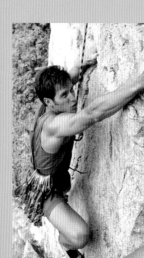

◀ Messages from the brain's movement area control this rock climber's muscles.

◀ These girls are using the right side of the brain to sing together.

speech area

vision area

sensory area

hearing area

cerebellum

Left and right

The largest part of the brain, called the cerebrum, is divided into two. The left half controls the right side of the body and helps you to solve problems, to speak and to write. The right half controls the body's left side and may help you to think about things that are hard to describe using words, such as music.

Heat control

Hidden deep inside the brain is an area called the hypothalamus. It is no bigger than the tip of your thumb. If the weather gets cold, the hypothalamus turns up your internal central heating. It also controls your appetite.

▼ The cerebrum is divided into areas that control different activities. This picture shows the right half of the cerebrum.

movement area

Auto pilot

As you concentrate on reading this book, hundreds of other activities are going on in your body. Breathing, digesting food and the beating of your heart are just a few of the things that are automatically controlled by your brain.

Coordination

At the back of the brain is a very wrinkly area, called the cerebellum. This helps you to keep your balance. The cerebellum also makes sure that your movements are smooth and not jerky.

▶ This chess player is using an area right at the front of his brain to work out his next move. This area is involved in problem solving.

thinking area

▼ The images that enter this boy's eyes through the telescope are turned into signals that are passed to an area at the back of the brain.

infolab

- Over 300 million nerve fibres connect the left and right sides of the brain together.

- 'Cerebellum' means 'little brain'.

Reflexes

The spinal cord is the main highway carrying information between the brain and the rest of the body. The spinal cord is packed with millions of nerve fibres and neurons, but it is more than just a pathway for messages. It also controls many automatic reactions in the body. These reactions are called reflexes.

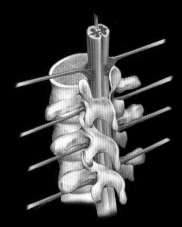

▲ The spinal cord (pink) is protected by the bones of the spine. Pairs of spinal nerves (green) connect the spinal cord to the rest of the body.

Action stations

Whenever the body needs to digest food, go to the toilet or speed up the heart, a special set of nerves from the spinal cord goes into action. These nerves automatically control many organs and glands.

◀ An automatic reaction, called the withdrawal reflex, allows this footballer to move his head out of the path of a fast-approaching ball.

◀ As soon as this girl touches the cactus, pain sensors in her skin send a signal to the spinal cord.

◀ Before the signal reaches her brain, the spinal cord has sent another signal back out to the muscles, pulling back the girl's arm.

In the tunnel

The spinal cord travels from your brain to just below your waist. The vertebrae, or bones of the spine, keep it safely in place. Nerves going to and from the rest of the body leave and enter the spinal cord through spaces between the bones.

Ouch!

Touch something very hot or very sharp and you will pull your hand away almost instantly. Your brain does not even have time to think about it! This reflex action can be controlled by the spinal cord without any help from the brain.

Knee jerk

Try testing one of your own reflexes. Sit on a desk with your legs dangling over the edge and ask a friend to gently tap just below your knee. Your leg should jerk upwards whether you want it to or not!

▲ A doctor tests the stretch reflex by tapping just below the kneecap. This reflex makes the muscle tighten and pull up the lower leg.

Spinal injury

Every year, many people injure their spinal cord in accidents. Damaged neurons cannot mend themselves, so a spinal injury can leave a person unable to walk or move.

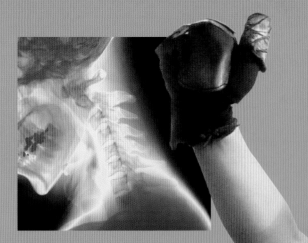

▲ This x-ray of the neck shows that the second vertebra down has been broken, causing a spinal injury.

Signal failure

If the spinal cord is damaged, signals may no longer be able to pass along the nerves to and from the brain. As a result, the person may lose the use of one or more limbs. This is called paralysis.

Wheel power!

Most people with severe spinal injuries need a wheelchair to get around. But this does not stop them from leading very active lives or playing wheelchair sports, which often require great skill.

In the future

Scientists are researching how to repair damaged neurons in the spinal cord. They have succeeded in growing neurons in the laboratory. One day, it may be possible to help people paralysed by a spinal injury to walk again.

◀ This picture, magnified 500 times, shows a neuron (yellow) growing on a computer chip. Such neurons may help paralysed people in the future.

▼ Wheelchair athletes use their hands to turn the wheels of their chair. This girl has trained hard to build up her upper body strength.

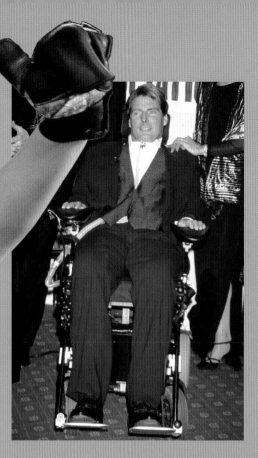

▲ Christopher Reeve, who played Superman, was paralysed in an accident. Before he died in 2004, he had begun to regain movement in different parts of his body.

Superman

Actor Christopher Reeve broke his neck in a horse riding accident. The injury to his spinal cord left him unable to move his arms or legs. He devoted the rest of his life to searching for a cure for paralysis and helping people with spinal injuries.

Vision

▲ In dim light, the pupil becomes as wide as possible (top) to let in light. In bright light, the pupil narrows to prevent too much light getting in.

A huge amount of information about the outside world comes to you through your eyes. The eye works like a camera, gathering in patterns of light from objects. These patterns are turned into signals. The brain uses the signals to create a picture of your surroundings.

In focus

As rays of light enter the eye, they are bent by the cornea. This starts to focus the light into a sharp image. The rays then pass through a clear lens that does the fine tuning, accurately focusing the picture onto the retina at the back of the eye.

Changing size

The pupil is a dark circular opening in the iris, or coloured part of the eye. It controls how much light reaches the back of the eye. The muscles of the iris make the pupil smaller so that you can see in bright light, or wider to help you see in poor light.

pupil

iris controls how much light enters the eye

lens changes shape to focus light

cornea lets light into eye

▲ The parts at the front of the eye focus light and control how much light enters. At the back, light is turned into signals, which are sent to the brain.

▲ When the light from an object is focused by the cornea and lens, the image appears upside down on the retina. The brain turns it the right way up.

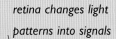

retina changes light
patterns into signals

optic nerve carries
signals to the brain

muscle controls
eyeball movement

▲ Millions of light-sensing rods (purple) and cones (orange) are packed into the retina.

Bit of a blur

If the eyeball is too short or too long, the eye cannot focus properly to produce a sharp image. The result is blurred vision and the person is said to be long sighted or short sighted. Wearing glasses or contact lenses corrects this very common problem.

Rods and cones

The retina is a layer of special cells at the back of the eye. These cells detect light and then send signals to the brain. Some cells, called cones, sense colours. Other light-detecting cells, called rods, can only detect black and white. In dim light, the cones do not work very well and the rods take over.

▶ A nearby object, such as this face, looks fuzzy to people who are long sighted. They cannot focus light properly onto the retina.

Tricking the brain

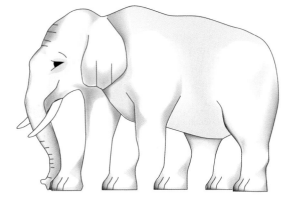

▲ How many legs does this elephant have? In trying to create a three-dimensional (3-D) image, your brain sees this image in more than one way.

Look closely at this page and prepare to have your brain boggled! When you look at an object, the brain must work out the patterns of light detected by your eyes. It is easy to trick the brain into seeing a picture in a certain way. These tricks are called optical illusions.

▼ Which is the bigger of the two central circles? If you think the circle on the right is bigger, you are wrong! They are actually the same size. Your brain is fooled by the size of the surrounding circles.

The third dimension

Our brains are used to seeing the world around us in three dimensions. But pictures printed or drawn on paper are only two-dimensional, as they have no depth. Even so, your brain can make it appear that you are looking at three dimensions.

▲ These rows appear to slope but, in fact, they are parallel. The brain is tricked by the uneven edges and the contrast between the black and white bricks.

▲ These identical twins are actually the same height, but the distorted shape of this Ames room tricks the brain. The girl on the left is much farther away than her sister.

Check again

The brain estimates the size of an object or shape by comparing it with other objects nearby. If a small object is surrounded by larger objects, the brain judges the smaller one to be less important. You will, in fact, see it as smaller than it really is.

Seeing isn't believing

Many optical illusions work by sending confusing information to the brain. Shapes can be made to move or shimmer and parallel lines can appear to bend. If a picture is not complete, the brain 'fills in' the missing information – but it does not always get it right!

Curiouser and curiouser

When you see a room, you expect it to be a regular shape. But in a special room called an Ames room, the floor and ceiling slope and the walls are sharply angled. A person moving from one corner to another will appear to shrink or to grow dramatically in size!

Hearing

Every noise, soft or loud, that reaches your ear is made up of sound waves. Inside the ear, the sound waves are turned into signals. These are sent to the brain, which lets you 'hear' the sound. Hearing helps us to communicate, to pick up warning signals and to enjoy good music!

▼ The ear has three main parts. The outer ear collects sounds. These pass through the middle ear and into the inner ear, which sends signals to the brain.

bones of the middle ear carry sound to the inner ear

inner ear

cochlea turns sound into signals

eardrum lies between the outer and middle ears

◀ Even a short burst of very loud noise can damage your hearing. In certain jobs it is very important to wear ear protectors.

Turn it down!

Your ears can detect the faintest of noises to the loudest of sounds. Sound is measured in decibels – a finger brushing over skin is around 10 decibels. The sound of a jet engine is a billion times louder and can measure over 130 decibels.

Good vibrations

Sound waves pass down the ear canal and make the eardrum vibrate. Behind the eardrum is the middle ear. Here, the vibrations of the eardrum are passed on through tiny bones that carry the sound across to the inner ear.

◀ Our hearing is so sensitive that we can pick up the quietest of whispers.

outer ear channels sound into the middle ear

infolab

- You can still hear sounds when you are asleep, but the brain ignores most of them.

- Each ear can clean itself! Tiny hairs push ear wax along and out of the ear canal to collect dirt.

- Sound waves travel through the air at 332m per second.

ear canal carries sound waves to the eardrum

▲ Sound waves arriving in the fluid-filled cochlea form ripples. These bend the tiny 'hairs' (yellow) which send signals to the brain.

Ripple effect

The main part of the inner ear, called the cochlea, forms a spiral chamber which is filled with fluid. Here, tiny ripples, caused by the vibrations in the middle ear, are turned into electrical signals. These are sent as messages down the hearing nerves to the brain.

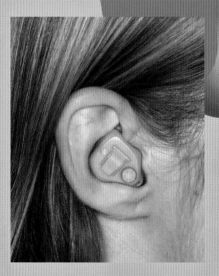

◀ If you have problems with your hearing you may need to wear a special device called a hearing aid.

Balance

If you want to dance, ride a bicycle or just stand upright, you need balance. In order to balance, the brain has to work out in which direction the body is moving. Much of this information is provided by your inner ear.

◀ Information from her eyes, ears and sense of touch helps this tightrope walker to stay balanced high above the ground.

Secret chambers

A system of chambers and canals, called the vestibular system, is found inside the inner ear. It detects the tiniest of changes in your body's position, and sends information to your brain. The brain can then adjust the muscles to control your balance.

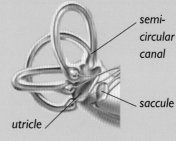

semi-
circular
canal

saccule

utricle

◀ The vestibular system is made up of semi-circular canals and jelly-filled chambers. Together, they help your brain detect the movement and position of your head.

▼ Tilting your head downwards bends tiny hairs in the utricle and saccule. This movement triggers signals that provide the brain with information about the head's position.

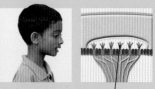

hairs stand upright   *hairs bend downwards*

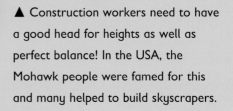

▲ Construction workers need to have a good head for heights as well as perfect balance! In the USA, the Mohawk people were famed for this and many helped to build skyscrapers.

Travel sickness

Sometimes your eyes and ears tell the brain two different things. If you have ever been seasick, it is usually because the balance organs in your ears tell the brain that your body is moving from side to side. But your eyes, which are looking at the deck, tell the brain that the boat is steady. This causes you to feel dizzy and sick.

▲ Seasickness is caused when the brain is confused by different information coming from the sense organs.

Use your eyes

Close your eyes and try standing on one leg. Not so easy, is it? This is because your brain uses information from the eyes as well as the ears when you want to balance.

Smell

Our noses sniff out the world around us, from freshly baked bread to a pair of old trainers. Each smell is made from a unique recipe of millions of tiny particles, or molecules, which float in the air. With every breath you take, these smell chemicals are carried into your nose. Here, they trigger sensors that send signals about the smell to the brain.

▲ Perfume makers can choose from up to 3,000 different plant and animal smells when they create a new fragrance.

Memory lane

Sometimes a particular smell can unlock old memories. This is because the nerves from our smell sensors are directly linked to the parts of the brain involved in storing memory.

Mood change

Smells can affect how you are feeling, because of links between the nose and the area of the brain that controls your emotions. Lavender, for example, has been found to help people relax when they are feeling stressed.

Warning system

You can detect at least 10,000 different smells. Your sense of smell can help to protect you from danger, by warning about leaking gas or rotten food.

◀ Dogs have many more smell detectors than humans and can pick up very faint smells.

◀ Smells can have powerful effects on the brain and body. Aromatherapists use perfumed oils to relax people and to treat health problems.

Smell experts

To make a perfume, dozens of different smells are combined together. Each perfume has its own individual scent. The highly trained expert who creates this is known as a 'nose'.

▼ Smells are picked up by sensors high up in the nose.

nerve carries signals to brain

smell molecules are breathed in through the nose

smell sensors

Taste

Imagine if everything you ate, from sweet, juicy oranges to chocolate ice cream, tasted of cardboard. Fortunately, your tongue has thousands of special taste sensors, or taste buds. Your tongue and lips can also detect heat, cold and the texture of food. These all add to the sensation and pleasure of eating.

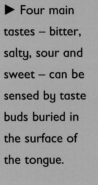

taste receptor

▲ Taste receptors are packed together inside a taste bud. They detect chemicals dissolved in saliva.

Bumpy surface

Look closely in a mirror at the surface of your tongue. The tiny lumps and bumps that cover it are known as papillae. These protect the delicate taste buds, which can be easily damaged. On the papillae are thousands of taste buds.

▶ Four main tastes – bitter, salty, sour and sweet – can be sensed by taste buds buried in the surface of the tongue.

bitter

salty

sour

sweet

A matter of smell

You need your sense of smell as well as your sense of taste to pick up the flavours in food. Your smell sensors are much more sensitive than your taste sensors. When you eat, the brain receives information from both sets of sensors.

▶ Thousands of tiny spikes on the surface of the tongue help to grip food. The pink bump, or papilla, is packed with taste buds.

Some like it hot

Some people love spicy foods such as chilli peppers. A chemical in the chilli pepper triggers pain sensors in the mouth. This sends signals to the brain that boost sweet flavours in the food and make it taste hot.

► Chilli peppers are a popular ingredient in many dishes because they boost the sweet flavours in food.

◄ Temperature sensors in the tongue tell the brain if the food you are eating is hot or cold.

Colour and taste

The colour of food can affect taste. Most people avoid blue or grey foods – we usually think of these colours as a sign of rotten or poisonous food. Food manufacturers often add artificial colouring to their products to make them look tastier.

Touch

▲ Babies often use their mouths to feel objects. The lips and tongue are packed with sensors and are extremely sensitive.

Close your eyes and touch the objects in front of you. Do they feel smooth or rough, cold or warm, soft or hard? Your sense of touch tells you a great deal about the world around you. Your skin is packed with millions of sensors that can detect tiny changes in movement, temperature and pressure. They can also sense pain.

Touch sensors

Some parts of the body are more sensitive to touch than others. The skin on the fingers and lips contains many more sensors than the skin on the back. Much more of the brain is used to detect touch signals from these sensitive areas than from other areas of the body.

▲ This is what your body would look like if the different parts were in proportion to the number of sensors they contain.

▲ This person is reading a Braille book. With practice, people can read Braille as fast as printed words.

The point of pain

Pain is not much fun, but it is a very good warning system that helps to prevent injury. For example, the eye's delicate covering, the cornea, is easily damaged, so even tiny flecks of dirt ring warning bells of pain.

Fingertip reading

Peope who are blind or partially sighted can use the Braille system to read. Special patterns formed by raised dots stand for each letter of the alphabet. People read the words by running their fingers over the dots.

The gentlest touch

Some of the skin's sensors are made of a bare nerve fibre wrapped around the base of a hair. These sensors can be triggered by the lightest touch, such as a feather brushing against hairs.

infolab

- One square centimetre of skin contains about 200 sensors for pain but only 15 for pressure.
- Braille was invented in France in 1824 by a blind 15-year-old boy called Louis Braille.

▼ Millions of microscopic sensors, of many different shapes and sizes, are buried under the skin.

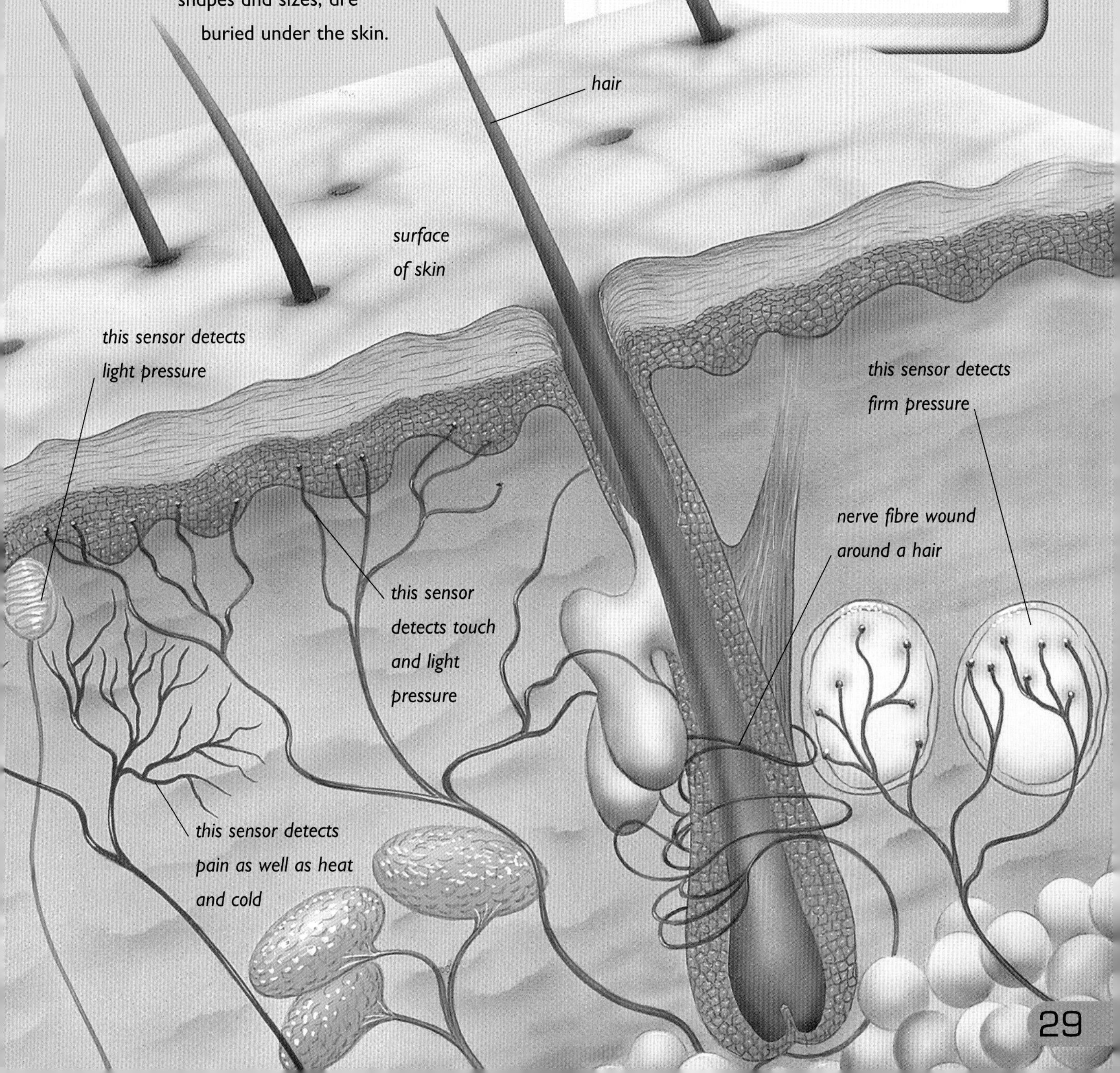

hair
surface of skin
this sensor detects light pressure
this sensor detects firm pressure
nerve fibre wound around a hair
this sensor detects touch and light pressure
this sensor detects pain as well as heat and cold

▲ Only human beings can think about and imagine their place in the universe.

Being human

The ability to think, to feel and to have a sense of who we are is very special to humans. This is often described as consciousness, and it makes us very different from other living creatures.

Feelings

When you get angry or feel happy, you are experiencing emotions – these are part of what makes us truly human. Emotions involve an area deep in the brain called the limbic system, which also deals with memory. Even so, no single area of the brain is linked with a specific emotion.

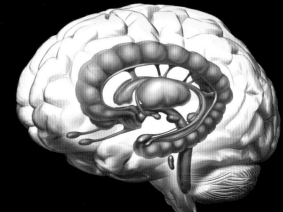

▲ The limbic system (blue) controls feelings such as pleasure, as well as memory.

The power of memory

Memory helps us to do simple tasks, such as riding a bicycle, as well as more complex things, such as speaking a foreign language. Memories are formed when links are made between the billions and billions of cells in our brains.

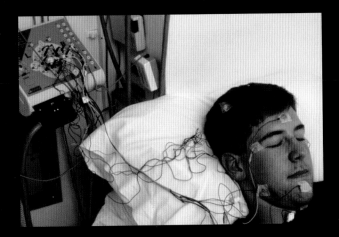

▲ While this man sleeps, a machine measures the electrical signals in his brain. No matter how deep the sleep, the brain is always active.

A good night's sleep

While the body rests every night, the brain switches from consciousness to a different state that we call sleep. Scientists still have much to learn about sleep. Dreams may be an attempt by the brain to order thoughts and feelings experienced during the day.

◀ The ability to play a musical instrument depends on skills that are learned over many years and stored in the memory.

Hormones

The nervous system is not the only route for messages to be sent around the body. A second system, called the endocrine system, uses chemical messages called hormones. These are in charge of growth, energy supply, reproduction and many other important activities.

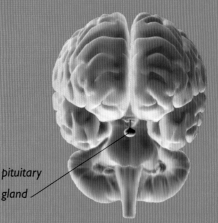

pituitary gland

▲ The pituitary gland is found just under the brain. It makes six different hormones and controls the release of other hormones.

Supply and demand

Hormones are made in small factories called the endocrine glands, which are found all around the body. Tiny amounts of the hormone are released into the bloodstream, when needed, to do their work a long way from the gland itself.

▶ The excitement and fear experienced when you ride a rollercoaster release adrenaline. This hormone prepares the body to face danger.

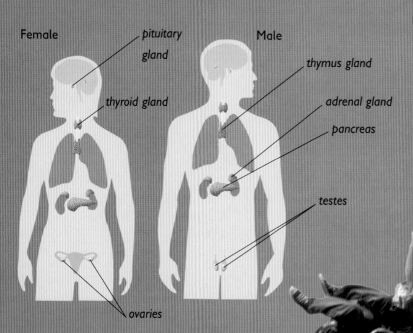

Female

pituitary gland

Male

thymus gland

thyroid gland

adrenal gland

pancreas

testes

ovaries

▲ The body makes more than 100 hormones. They are produced in the endocrine glands, which are found in different parts of the body.

The master gland

Just below the brain is a small but very important gland called the pituitary gland. The pituitary gland makes growth hormone – without this chemical, your body would not grow.

infolab

- Hormones travel much more slowly than messages carried by the nerves.

- Laughter can lower your levels of stress hormones.

- The pituitary gland is joined to the hypothalamus – the part of the brain that controls body temperature.

Under pressure

If the body is put under stress, it produces adrenaline. This hormone makes the heart beat faster, sending more blood to the muscles and brain. It also speeds up breathing and releases sugar into the blood for energy.

▲ Hormones control puberty – the period when children begin to develop into adults.

Mind over matter

Sometimes, in extreme situations, the brain can drive the body past its normal limits, overcoming hunger, pain, weakness or exhaustion. With practice we can also use our minds to relax our bodies, control our fears and even keep illness at bay.

◄ This boy uses his mind to remain calm and keep his body still as a large spider crawls up his arm.

Phobias

Many people suffer from phobias, or irrational fears. There are all kinds of phobias, from a fear of spiders to a fear of flying. Hypnotism, in which the person is put into a trance, is often used to help people with phobias.

◄ Overcoming extreme pain is a sign of religious devotion in some cultures. Here, an Indian man is standing on nails.

The pain barrier

One of the greatest challenges for the brain is to ignore pain. Many cultures have rituals or festivals that involve acts in which people must test their limits – by lying on a bed of nails, for example.

Ancient practice

For over 5,000 years, people have practised yoga to stay well. Yoga uses meditation in order to focus the mind. Most people find it very relaxing, and it can even help to keep your heart in good shape.

◀ This Indian man is practising yoga to enter into a very calm state and clear his mind of distractions.

Remote control

A scientist called Andrew Junker has steered a boat by thought alone! A special headband picks up electrical signals from his brain and sends them to a computer that controls the steering.

▶ The performer David Blaine stood inside a block of ice for over 60 hours. He used meditation to withstand extreme cold, exhaustion and hunger.

Glossary

adrenaline A hormone that prepares the body to face danger by speeding up the heart, sending more blood to the muscles and releasing sugar for energy.

brain The part of the nervous system that is enclosed inside the skull. The brain is the control centre of the body.

cerebellum The area at the back of the brain that controls balance and co-ordinates movement.

cochlea A snail-shaped part of the inner ear where sound vibrations are turned into nerve signals and sent to the brain.

cornea A transparent layer at the front of the eye. The cornea works with the lens to focus light onto the retina.

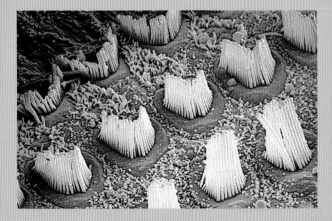

eardrum A part of the ear that vibrates when sound waves reach it. It separates the middle ear from the outer ear.

endocrine system The system of glands around the body that makes chemical messages called hormones and releases them into the bloodstream.

hormones Chemicals produced by glands. Hormones pass around the body in the bloodstream to specific areas or organs. Hormones control how other cells or organs work.

iris The coloured ring at the front of the eye. It controls the size of the pupil.

lens A transparent disc in the eye that focuses rays of light onto the retina.

limbic system An area of the brain that controls emotions and memory.

nerve A string-like bundle of nerve cells that carries information between the nervous system and the rest of the body.

nerve fibre A thread-like part of a nerve cell. Electrical signals pass along the nerve fibres, which may be just a few millimetres or up to a metre in length.

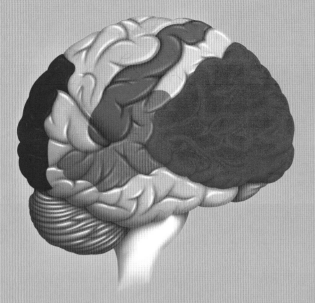

retina The lining of the eyeball. Light falling onto the retina forms images which are turned into electrical signals and sent to the brain.

sense organ A part of the body, such as the eye, ear or skin, that sends information about the outside world to the brain.

spinal cord The part of the nervous system packed with neurons that runs from the brain down the backbone.

nervous system The network of nerve cells that carries information around the body, and controls many of the body's activities. The brain is the nervous system's headquarters.

neuron A nerve cell that carries signals at high speed around the body.

spine A flexible, strong column of bone, made of 33 bones called vertebrae. It forms a protective tunnel for the spinal cord, and is also known as the spinal column or the backbone.

optic nerve A bundle of neurons that carries information from the retina, at the back of the eye, to the brain.

taste bud A small cluster of sensors that detect taste chemicals in saliva. Taste buds are found in the tongue's surface.

pupil The circular opening in the centre of the iris, through which light rays pass into the eye.

vertebrae The 33 irregular-shaped bones that are piled on top of each other to form the spinal column.

reflex An automatic reaction, often in response to danger.

Index

Websites

The Kidshealth website has loads of fascinating facts about the brain:
www.kidshealth.org/kid/body/brain_SW.html

Put your senses to the challenge or wire up your nervous system with the help of these interactive games on the BBC website:
www.bbc.co.uk/science/humanbody/body/index_interactivebody.shtml

The Laurent Clerc National Deaf Education Centre has lots of quizzes and information on hearing:
http://clerccenter.gallaudet.edu/InfoToGo/567/567.html

For more on your senses, explore the Neuroscience for Kids website:
http://faculty.washington.edu/chudler/chsense.html

Visit the Eye Site to learn about vision:
http://library.thinkquest.org/J002330/?tqskip1=1

Test your reflexes with the fastball reaction challenge:
www.exploratorium.edu/baseball/reactiontime.html

This site is a good introducton to the endocrine system:
http://yucky.kids.discovery.com/noflash/body/pg000133.html

Acknowledgements

The publisher would like to thank the following for permission to reproduce their material. Every care has been taken to trace copyright holders. However, if there have been unintentional omissions or failure to trace copyright holders, we apologise and will, if informed, endeavour to make corrections in any future edition.

Key: b = bottom, c = centre, l = left, r = right, t = top

Cover tl Getty; cl Science Photo Library (SPL); c Getty Imagebank; br Corbis; page 1 SPL; 2–3 Corbis; 4–5 Corbis; 6tl Getty Taxi; 6bl Corbis; 6cr Alamy; 7l Getty Rubberball Productions; 7r The Art Archive; 8tl SPL; 8bl Corbis; 9br SPL; 10tr Corbis; 10cl Getty Taxi; 11bl Getty Stone; 11r Getty Imagebank; 12 Getty Photodisc Green; 13 Alamy; 14 SPL; 14–15 Getty Taxi; 15tr Corbis; 16 SPL; 17c SPL; 17br Getty Stone; 19 Exploratorium; 20cl Getty Stone; 20bl Corbis; 21cr SPL; 21bl Getty Imagebank; 22–23 Alamy; 23tr Getty Stone; 23c SPL; 24cl Corbis; 24b Getty Imagebank; 24–25 Alamy; 25 Corbis; 26 Robert Harding; 27l Getty Stone; 27r Getty Stone; 28tl Corbis; 28cr Alamy; 30tl SPL; 30–31 Corbis; 31cl SPL; 32tr SPL; 32–33 Corbis; 33 Corbis; 34l Corbis; 34bc Corbis; 35cl Getty Imagebank; 35r Corbis; 36 SPL; 37 Getty Imagebank; poster bl Corbis; c Getty